indian
rice and breads

Devagi Sanmugam

A delicious collection of Indian rice and breads
that you can prepare in your own kitchen.

PERIPLUS

Basic Indian Ingredients

Asafoetida is a pungent gum which is usually sold in powdered form. Use very small amounts—a pinch is enough. Keep well sealed when not in use.

Atta flour is a form of whole wheat flour. It is made from durum wheat that is ground very fine, with some of the bran included. Breads made from atta flour include chapati and roti.

Basmati rice is an Indian long-grain rice variety characterised by its thinness and fragrance. The grains stay whole and separate when cooked. Substitute long-grain Thai jasmine rice.

Chillies are indispensable in Asian cooking. The usual red and green finger-length chillies are moderately hot. Dried chillies are usually cut in lengths and soaked in warm water to soften before use. **Chilli powder,** a crucial ingredient in Indian cooking, is made from ground chillies.

Cardamom pods are highly aromatic and contain tiny black seeds. If whole pods are used, they should be removed from the food before serving. If seeds are called for, lightly smash the pods and remove the seeds, discarding the pods. Ground cardamon is sold in packets or tins.

Coconut milk is made by mixing freshly grated coconut flesh (available from Asian markets) with water and squeezing the liquid from the mixture. Add 125 ml ($1/2$ cup) water to 3 cups of grated fresh coconut. Squeeze and strain to obtain **thick coconut milk**. Add 625 ml ($2^1/2$ cups) water to the grated coconut and squeeze again to obtain **thin coconut milk**. Cans or packets of concentrated coconut milk make a good substitute; dilute according to the instructions.

Coriander is a pungent herb and spice plant that is essential in Asian cooking. **Coriander leaves,** also known as cilantro or Chinese parsley, are sold in small bunches with the roots intact. They are used as a herb and a garnish. Small, round **coriander seeds** are slightly citrusy in fragrance and are used whole or ground in curry pastes and spice mixes.

Bengal dal (Channa dal)

White gram or ural dal

Bengal gram or channa dal resembles a yellow split pea but is smaller. Bengal gram is also ground to make **Bengal flour**. **White gram** is husked urad dal and is sold either with its black skin on, or husked when it is creamy white in colour.

Cumin seeds (*jeera*) are pale brown and usually partnered with coriander seeds in basic spice mixes. They impart an intense, earthy flavour to foods and are often dry-roasted or flash-cooked in oil to intensify their flavour.

Curry leaves are sold in sprigs containing 8–15 small, green leaves and are used to flavour Indian curries. There is no good substitute.

Curry powder is a readily available blend of Indian spices, and typically contains turmeric, coriander, chillies, cumin, mustard, ginger, fenugreek, garlic, cloves, salt, and any number of other spices.

Garam masala is an Indian blend of powdered spices, usually including cinnamon, cardamon, cloves, fennel and black pepper. Pre-blended garam masala can be bought from any store specializing in spices. Store in an airtight jar away from heat or sunlight.

Fennel seeds look like cumin seeds but are larger and paler. They add a sweet fragrance to Indian dishes, with a flavour similar to liquorice or anise. The seeds are used whole or ground.

Ghee is a rich clarified butter oil with the milk solids removed that is the main oil used in Indian cooking. Substitute with vegetable oil or butter.

Lentils are protein- and fibre-rich legumes that feature prominently in Indian cuisine. **Mung lentils** are small, flattish yellow beans that are easy to cook and need no soaking. **Red lentils** are dark brown or almost greenish black in colour when whole. Split red lentils have a pinkish orange centre and are used in curries.

Mustard seeds are small brownish-black seeds that are commonly used in Indian cooking, imparting a nutty flavour to dishes.

Saffron is the world's most expensive spice. The dried strands should be allowed to infuse in warm milk before being added to rice and dessert dishes. Store saffron in the freezer as it loses its fragrance quickly, and never buy powdered saffron if you want the true aroma of this spice.

Tamarind is commonly available in the form of semi-dried pulp. It must be soaked in water, mashed, squeezed and strained to yield a sour juice that is added to soups and sauces. All solids and pulp should be strained and discarded from the liquid before use.

Turmeric resembles ginger when fresh but is commonly sold in dried form as a yellow powder. Turmeric turns dishes yellow and has a mild flavour.

Date Chutney

1 kg (2 lb) pitted dates, chopped
500 g (1 lb) spring onions, chopped
375 g (12 oz) raisins
125 g ($^2/_3$ cup) caster sugar
2 tablespoons salt
1 tablespoon garam masala
1$^1/_2$ teaspoons chilli powder
1 tablespoon mustard seeds, pounded coarsely
1 litre (4 cups) white vinegar

Serves 4
Preparation time: **5 mins**
Cooking time: **30 mins**

1 Put all the above ingredients into a thick-bottomed pan and cook over medium heat for about 30 minutes or until the chutney thickens.
2 Cool it thoroughly and store in sterilised jars.
3 Serve with any of the bread dishes or rice dishes.

Peanut Chutney

4 tablespoons grated coconut
80 g ($^2/_3$ cup) unsalted peanuts, roasted
4 cm (1$^1/_2$ in) ginger peeled and chopped
4 tablespoons fresh coriander (cilantro) leaves,
  finely chopped
4 green chillies, chopped
2 medium onions, chopped
125 ml ($^1/_2$ cup) water
2 tablespoons oil
1 teaspoon mustard seeds
1 sprig curry leaves
$^1/_4$ teaspoon asafoetida powder
$^1/_4$ teaspoon salt

Serves 4
Preparation time: **15 mins**
Cooking time: **5 mins**

1 Combine coconut, peanuts, ginger, coriander, chillies, onions and water in a blender and blend until smooth. Transfer to a bowl and set aside.
2 Heat oil in a small pan over medium heat and add the mustard seeds; when it splutters add the curry leaves and asafoetida powder and fry until fragrant. Remove from the heat and pour this over the ground chutney.
3 Stir in the salt and serve with *thosai* or *idli*. Consume within 3 hours or keep refrigerated for up to 1 day.

Onion Chutney

2 large onions, 400 g (14 oz), coarsely chopped
2 cm (1 in) ginger, chopped
3 green chillies
4 tablespoons lemon/lime juice
2 tablespoons oil
1 dried red chilli, cut into 2-cm (1-in) pieces
1 teaspoon cumin seeds
1 teaspoon salt

Serves 4
Preparation time: **10 mins**
Cooking time: **3 mins**

1 Combine the onions, ginger, chillies and lemon or lime juice in a blender until smooth.
2 Heat oil over medium heat and fry the dried chilli until browned, then add the cumin seeds. When it stops spluttering pour over the ground ingredients, add salt and mix well.
3 Serve with *thosai* or *idli*. Consume within 5 hours or keep refrigerated for up to 1 day.

Spinach Chutney

300 g (10 oz) spinach, washed and chopped, steamed and cooled
80 g ($^1/_4$ cup) sesame seeds, dry roasted
150 g (1$^1/_4$ cups) roasted peanuts
4 green chillies
1 teaspoon salt
1 tablespoon tamarind paste, seeds discarded
2 tablespoons oil
$^1/_4$ teaspoon mustard seeds
$^1/_4$ teaspoon cumin seeds
1 onion, sliced
2 sprigs curry leaves

Serves 4
Preparation time: **20 mins**
Cooking time: **3 mins**

1 Combine cooled spinach, sesame seeds, peanuts, green chillies, salt and tamarind paste in a blender and blend until smooth.
2 Heat oil in a pan over medium heat and fry the mustard and cumin seeds until they stop spluttering. Add the curry leaves and onion slices and sauté until the onions soften and brown lightly.
3 Transfer to the ground ingredients; mix well and serve with any breads, *thosai*, *idli* or rice dishes as an accompaniment. Consume within 5 hours or keep refrigerated for up to 1 day.

Mysore Idli

150 g (1 cup) split white gram, soaked for 5 hours, drained
430 ml (1³/₄ cups) water
400 g (2¹/₂ cups) rice semolina (*idli rava*), soaked in plenty of water for 20 minutes
3 teaspoons salt
100 g (³/₄ cup) carrot, diced
100 g (³/₄ cup) potato, peeled and diced
50 g (¹/₄ cup) peas
1 teaspoon turmeric powder

1 Blend drained white gram with water until smooth. Transfer to a deep pot.
2 Wash soaked rice semolina in several changes of water and drain well. Squeeze out all the excess water. Mix the drained rice semolina with the blended white gram. Add salt and mix well.
3 Cover and leave to ferment at room temperature (about 28°C) for at least 12 hours or overnight. If the batter is fermented on a relatively warm day, you may have to reduce standing time.
4 Before steaming the *idli*, mix all the ingredients thoroughly.
5 Line *idli* steaming rack with a wet muslin cloth. Fill the moulds with batter. Place in steamer, cover and steam over high heat for 15 minutes.
6 Serve with coconut chutney or curry.

If you cannot find an idli steamer, pour batter into greased porcelain cups about 7 cm (3 in) wide and 4 cm (1¹/₂ in) high. Steam for 15 minutes or microwave covered for 5 minutes.

Makes 10 pieces
Soaking time: **5 hours**
Preparation time: **30 mins**
Fermentation time: **12 hours**
Cooking time: **15 mins**

Stuffed Sweet Idli

Batter
180 g (1 cup) parboiled rice
220 g (1 cup) plain rice
135 g (³/₄ cup) *urad* dhal or white gram
125 ml (1 cup) water
¹/₄ teaspoon salt

Filling
1 tablespoon ghee
240 g (2 cups) grated coconut
6 tablespoons caster sugar
2 tablespoons cashew nuts, roasted and chopped
1 tablespoon sesame seeds, roasted and pounded coarsely
1 tablespoon groundnuts, roasted and pounded
8 cardamoms, pods discarded and seeds ground until powdery

1 To make the batter, soak both types of rice and dhal together for 6 hours. Blend the rice and dhal with the water to form a smooth paste. Add salt and stir well.
2 Cover and set aside for 10 hours to ferment at room temperature (28°C). If the batter is fermented on a relatively warm day, you may have to reduce standing time.
3 To make the filling, heat ghee over medium heat and fry coconut for 4 to 5 minutes, until golden brown. Add the rest of the ingredients and mix well.
4 Lightly grease *idli* moulds or shallow cups, (see page 6 for alternative method) with ghee. Pour in a little batter. Put about 3 teaspoons of the filling over it and cover with batter again. Steam for 15 to 20 minutes.

Makes 12 pieces
Soaking time: **6 hours**
Preparation time: **1 hour**
Fermentation time: **10 hours**
Cooking time: **30 mins**

Kanchipuram Idli

2 tablespoons ghee
1 teaspoon mustard seeds
80 g ($^1/_2$ cup) cashew nuts, roughly chopped
210 g (1$^1/_4$ cups) semolina
2 cm ($^3/_4$ in) ginger, finely minced
2 green chillies, finely chopped
1 sprig curry leaves, shredded
3 tablespoons finely chopped fresh coriander
   (cilantro) leaves
1$^1/_4$ teaspoons salt
500 ml (2 cups) yoghurt
$^1/_4$ teaspoon bicarbonate of soda

1 Heat ghee in a pan over medium heat. Add mustard seeds and cashew pieces and fry until golden brown, about 1 minute.
2 Add semolina and fry over medium heat for 3 minutes then remove from heat and cool.
3 In a mixing bowl, combine cooled semolina, ginger, chillies, curry leaves, coriander and salt.
4 Whisk yoghurt lightly until smooth before mixing with bicarbonate of soda and the semolina mix. Mix the batter lightly, you should see bubbles coming from the batter.
5 Line an *idli* steaming rack with a wet muslin cloth. Fill the moulds with batter (see page 6 for alternative method).
6 Place in the steamer, cover and steam for 15 minutes over high heat.
7 Serve with dhal curry or chutney.

Serves 4
Preparation time: **40 mins**
Cooking time: **20 mins**

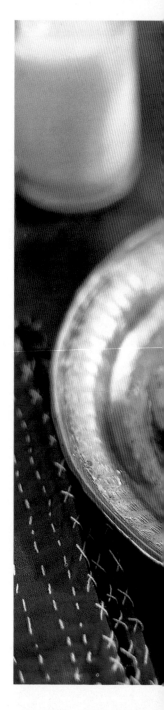

White or Brown Rice String Hoppers
(Idiappam)

300 g (2¼ cups) rice flour, brown rice flour or millet (also known as ragi or rye) flour
1¼ teaspoon salt
500 ml (2 cups) boiling water
Grated coconut and brown or orange sugar for garnish

Makes 8 pieces
Preparation time: **15 mins**
Cooking time: **10 mins**

1 Place flour on a dry cloth and steam over high heat for 10 minutes. Cool thoroughly and sift into a mixing bowl.
2 Dissolve salt in hot water and add the water to the flour. Using a wooden spoon, stir quickly to form a soft dough.
3 Put a little dough into an *idiappam* press. Press dough out into long strands to form a circle on a rattan plate or lightly greased saucer. Repeat procedure until dough is finished—you can form several circles on larger saucers or use a number of smaller saucers.
4 Place prepared *idiappam* in steamer. Steam for 10 minutes or until *idiappam* turns slightly translucent and texture is firm.
5 Garnish with grated coconut and brown and orange sugar. *Idiappam* can also be served with chicken or vegetable curry.

Spoon the dough into an iddiapam *press, then lightly grease a saucer.*

Press dough out into long strands forming a circle on the greased saucer.

Coconut Appam

1 tablespoon cooked rice
250 ml (1 cup) warm water
1 1/2 cups (180 g) rice flour
1 teaspoon instant yeast
2 teaspoons sugar
1/4 teaspoon salt
375 ml (1 1/2 cups) thick coconut milk (add 100 ml
  or 1/3 cup water if using canned or packet coconut)

1 Blend the cooked rice and warm water until smooth. Transfer to a mixing bowl and add the rice flour, yeast, sugar and salt. Mix until it forms a thick, smooth batter.
2 Cover and set aside for 4 hours to ferment at room temperature (28°C). If the batter is fermented on a relatively warm day, you may have to reduce standing time.
3 Add the coconut milk and mix to form a slightly watery batter. Set aside for 2 hours.
4 Heat an *appam* wok and grease it lightly with oil.
5 Pour 3 to 4 tablespoons of the batter into the wok. Rotate the wok by hand so that about 3 cm (1 1/5 in) of the side of the wok is thinly coated and the remaining batter collects at the centre. Care should be taken that it is rotated only twice. Cover with a tight fitting lid.
6 Lower heat and cook about 3 minutes or until set and the edges resemble crisp lace, the centre is soft and well-risen and the underneath is golden brown.
7 Serve with mutton, fish or chicken curry. This dish can also be eaten with brown sugar.

Instead of an appam wok, you can also use a small Chinese wok about 14 cm (5 1/2 in) in diameter.

Serves 4
Preparation time: **20 mins**
Fermentation time: **4 hours**
Resting time: **2 hours**
Cooking time: **15 mins**

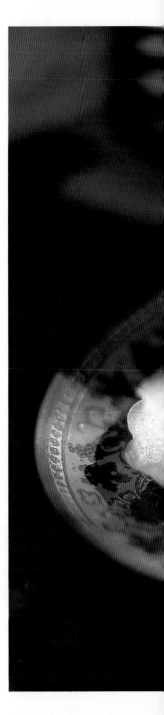

Banana Appam

440 g (2 cups) rice, soaked for 4–5 hours, drained
40 g (scant $^1/_2$ cup) grated coconut
1 ripe banana, about 125 g (4 oz)
125 ml ($^1/_2$ cup) coconut water
$^1/_2$ teaspoon salt
$^1/_2$ teaspoon bicarbonate of soda

1 Blend the rice, coconut, banana and coconut water into a satiny smooth paste.
2 Add the salt and set aside, covered, for 5 hours to ferment at room temperature (28°C). If the batter is fermented on a relatively warm day, you may have to reduce standing time.
3 Add the sodium bicarbonate and mix well. Add a little water if needed. The batter should flow freely off a spoon.
4 Heat a frying pan over medium-low heat, and grease it lightly. Pour a ladle of batter into the pan, spreading it like a thick pancake. Cover the pan with a lid. Cook until the underside is browned, 8 to 10 minutes
5 Serve hot with coconut chutney, coconut milk or brown sugar.

Makes 6 pieces
Preparation time: **20 mins**
Fermentation time: **5 hours**
Cooking time: **1 hour**

Potato Rice

2 tablespoons ghee
6 cm ($2^1/_2$ in) cinnamon stick, broken in two
4 cloves
4 cardamoms
2 bay leaves
300 g ($1^1/_2$ cups) Basmati rice or long grain rice,
   washed and drained
600 ml ($2^1/_3$ cups) water
300 g ($1^3/_4$ cups) peeled potatoes, diced
1 teaspoon turmeric powder
$^1/_2$ teaspoon chilli powder
$^1/_2$ teaspoon garam masala
$1^1/_4$ teaspoon salt

1 Heat the ghee over medium heat and fry the
cinnamon, cloves, cardamoms and bay leaves until
aromatic. Add the drained rice and stir fry for
1 minute. Turn off heat.
2 Bring water, potatoes, turmeric powder, chilli
powder, garam masala and salt to the boil . After it has
boiled for 3 minutes, add the rice. Lower the heat and
cook until the rice is cooked, about 10 to 15 minutes.
Remove whole spices and serve.

Serves 2
Preparation time: **10 mins**
Cooking time: **25 mins**

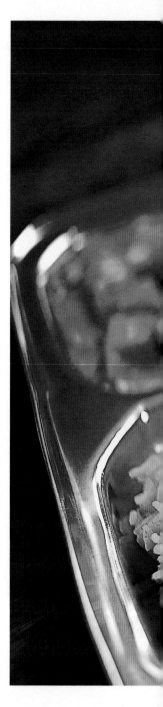

Tamarind Rice

375 g (3 cups) cooked rice, cooled thoroughly
5 tablespoons Indian sesame oil
1 teaspoon turmeric powder
$1/_2$ teaspoon chilli powder
1 teaspoon cumin seeds
$1/_4$ teaspoon fenugreek seeds
1 teaspoon Bengal gram
1 teaspoon white gram
1 teaspoon mustard seeds
2 dried chillies, cut into 3-cm ($1^1/_4$-in) pieces
2 sprigs curry leaves
50 g ($1^2/_3$ oz) tamarind pulp, mixed with 100 ml (scant $1/_2$ cup) water and strained
$1^1/_4$ teaspoons salt
$1/_4$ teaspoon asafoetida powder
2 tablespoons white sesame seeds, roasted until light brown and coarsely pounded

1 Mix rice and 2 tablespoons of the sesame oil together thoroughly and set aside for 1 hour.

2 Heat a small pan over low heat and dry-roast turmeric and chilli powders until fragrant, about 2 minutes. Set aside.

3 Dry roast cumin and fenugreek until fragrant, about 2 minutes. Grind to a fine powder using a coffee grinder. Set aside.

4 Heat remaining sesame oil over medium heat. Add Bengal gram and white gram. Fry until golden brown, about 2 minutes. Add mustard seeds, dried chillies and curry leaves. Fry until the mustard seeds pop. Add tamarind water, salt, asafoetida powder and the roasted ground spice powders from steps 2 and 3.

5 Bring to the boil over medium heat for 3 to 4 minutes then remove from heat. Pour over the prepared rice, sprinkle with roasted sesame seeds and mix well. Set aside for 1 hour before serving.

Serves 4
Preparation time: **15 mins**
Cooking time: **15 mins**
Resting time: **1 hour**

Sesame Rice

1 tablespoon oil
1 teaspoon white gram
4 dried chillies, cut into
  1-cm ($^1/_2$-in) pieces
3 tablespoons white
  sesame seeds, roasted
  until aromatic
1 teaspoon salt
2 tablespoons Indian
  sesame oil
$^1/_2$ teaspoon mustard
  seeds
2 sprigs curry leaves
375 g (3 cups) hot or
  warm cooked rice

1 Heat oil over medium heat and fry the white gram and the dried chillies for about 2 minutes, until the gram turns golden brown. Remove from oil.
2 Grind the white gram, dried chillies, sesame seeds and salt to a powder.
3 Heat sesame oil over medium heat and fry the mustard seeds and curry leaves for 2 to 3 minutes, until aromatic and the seeds splutter.
4 Transfer the ground ingredients and the fried ingredients to the rice. Mix well and serve. This dish can be served warm, hot or at room temperature.

Serves 4
Preparation time: **10 mins**
Cooking time: **15 mins**

Peanut Rice

3 tablespoons grated coconut

1 teaspoon turmeric powder

1 teaspoon chilli powder

100 g (scant 1 cup) roasted, unsalted peanuts, coarsely pounded

1 teaspoon white sesame seeds

1 teaspoon salt

375 g (3 cups) hot or warm cooked rice

2 tablespoons oil

$^1/_2$ teaspoon mustard seeds

1 teaspoon white gram

2 teaspoons Bengal gram

2 sprigs curry leaves

1 In a pan, over low heat, dry roast the grated coconut, turmeric powder and the chilli powder until the coconut becomes dry, about 3 minutes.

2 Mix the pounded peanuts, sesame seeds, dry roasted ingredients and salt together. Then mix all these ingredients into the rice.

3 Heat oil and fry the mustard seeds until they pop. Add the white gram and the Bengal gram dhal and fry until golden brown, about 2 minutes. Add the curry leaves and when it becomes aromatic, transfer to the rice and mix well. This dish can be served warm, hot or at room temperature.

Serves 4
Preparation time: **15 mins**
Cooking time: **10 mins**

Coconut Rice

375 g (3 cups) hot or warm cooked rice
1 tablespoon melted ghee
1 teaspoon salt
2 tablespoons oil
1 teaspoon Bengal gram
1 teaspoon white gram
$^1/_2$ teaspoon mustard seeds
3 dried chillies, cut into 3-cm (1$^1/_4$-in) pieces
2 green chillies, sliced
2 sprigs curry leaves
100 g (1 cup) grated fresh coconut
2 tablespoons finely chopped fresh coriander
  (cilantro) leaves
3 tablespoons roasted cashew nuts, broken into
  small pieces

1 Put cooked rice, ghee and salt into a bowl and mix well. Set aside while preparing the rest of the dish.
2 Heat oil and fry the Bengal gram and white gram over medium heat until golden brown, about 2 to 3 minutes. Add the mustard seeds and dried chillies, and fry until the seeds pop and chillies turn brown, about 1 to 2 minutes, taking care not to burn the chillies.
3 Add the green chillies and curry leaves and stir fry until really aromatic, about another 2 minutes, then add the coconut, coriander leaves and cashew nuts. Stir to mix well and remove from heat.
4 Mix into the prepared rice thoroughly. Serve warm or at room temperature.

Serves 4
Preparation time: **15 mins**
Cooking time: **10 mins**

Sweet Saffron Rice

3 tablespoons ghee
6 cm (2$^1/_2$ in) cinnamon
  stick, broken in half
4 cloves
250 ml (1 cup) milk
Pinch of saffron, toasted
  lightly and crushed
220 g (1 cup) caster sugar
375 g (3 cups) hot or
  warm cooked Basmati
  rice or long grain rice
$^1/_2$ teaspoon ground
  cardamom
2 tablespoons chopped
  pistachio nuts
2 tablespoons chopped
  blanched and roasted
  almonds
2 tablespoons raisins

1 Heat ghee over medium heat and fry the cinnamon and cloves until aromatic, about 1 to 2 minutes.
2 Add the milk, saffron and sugar and boil until sugar dissolves and the saffron has coloured the milk, about 3 minutes.
3 Add the rice and cardamom, and simmer, covered, until the milk has been absorbed by the rice, about 10 minutes. Turn off the heat and stir in the nuts, almonds and raisins. Serve hot or at room temperature as a snack or a dessert.

Serves 5
Preparation time: **15 mins**
Cooking time: **15 mins**

Jeera Rice

2 tablespoons ghee or butter
100 g (³/₄ cup) roasted cashew nuts
1 tablespoon cumin seeds
8 cm (3 in) cinnamon stick, broken in half
5 cardamoms
5 cloves
3 tablespoons onion paste
2 teaspoons ginger paste
2 teaspoons garlic paste
300 g (1¹/₂ cups) Basmati rice or long grain rice, washed and drained
500 ml (2 cups) water
1 teaspoon salt

1 Heat ghee in a pan over medium heat. Add cashew nuts and fry until golden brown. Remove nuts and set aside.
2 Add cumin seeds, cinnamon, cardamoms and cloves to the pan. Fry for 1 minute, then add the onion, ginger and garlic pastes and fry for another 2 minutes.
3 Add rice and stir fry for about 1 minute.
4 Bring water to the boil in a pan. Add the salt and rice mixture. Stir to mix well. Cook over low flame until rice is done. Garnish with roasted cashew nuts before serving.

Serves 4
Preparation time: **10 mins**
Cooking time: **15 mins**

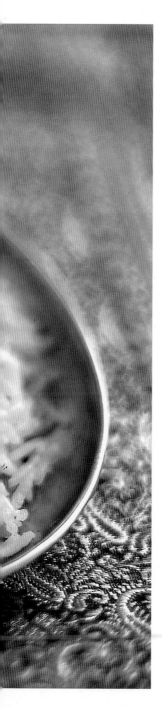

Mango Rice

2 tablespoons ghee or oil
1 tablespoon Bengal gram
1 tablespoon white gram
$^1/_2$ teaspoon mustard seeds
3 dried chillies, cut into 3-cm (1$^1/_4$-in) pieces
2 green chillies, sliced
2 sprigs curry leaves
1 teaspoon turmeric powder
250 g ($^1/_4$ lb) unripe green mango, peeled, stoned
  and grated
1$^1/_2$ teaspoons salt
375 g (3 cups) hot or warm cooked rice
2 tablespoons chopped fresh coriander (cilantro) leaves

1 Heat ghee in a pan over medium heat, and fry
Bengal and white gram until golden brown, about
2 to 3 minutes,
2 Add the mustard seeds and dried chillies and sauté
for another 2 to 3 minutes, until the dried chillies
turn brown. Add in the green chillies, curry leaves and
turmeric powder. Sauté for about 2 minutes over low
heat, then add in the grated mango, salt and the
cooked rice. Stir fry for about 5 minutes and remove
from heat.
3 Serve garnished with chopped coriander leaves.

Serves 5
Preparation time: **10 mins**
Cooking time: **8 mins**

Hyderabad Chicken Biryani

Chicken

1 teaspoon fennel seeds
1 teaspoon white
  peppercorns
1 teaspoon cumin seeds
$1/2$ teaspoon cardamom
  seeds
1 kg (2 lb) chicken,
  skinned and cut into
  serving size pieces
4 tablespoons ginger
  paste
4 tablespoons garlic
  paste
100 ml ($1/2$ cup) yoghurt
$1 1/2$ teaspoon salt
2 tablespoons ghee
6 cm ($2 1/2$ in) cinnamon
  stick, broken in half
5 cloves
5 cardamoms
2 bay leaves
3 green chillies, slit
  lengthwise
4 onions, thinly sliced
2 large ripe tomatoes,
  finely chopped
1 teaspoon turmeric
  powder
1 teaspoon chilli powder
$1 1/2$ tablespoon
  coriander powder
$1/2$ teaspoon nutmeg
  powder

*If you prefer a more
spicy rice mixture, add
one or two sliced green
chillies when cooking
the rice. Alternatively,
you can serve the
chicken separately from
the rice.*

Rice

3 tablespoons ghee
5 cm (2 in) cinnamon
  stick, broken in half
5 cardamoms
5 cloves
1 star anise
1 bay leaf
500 g ($2 1/4$ cups) basmati
  rice, washed and drained
100 ml ($1/2$ cup) yoghurt
1 teaspoon yellow
  colouring or a pinch of
  saffron, crushed
$1 1/4$ teaspoons salt
1 tablespoon rose water
1 litre (4 cups) water or
  chicken stock

Garnish

2 tablespoons raisins,
  fried until puffed up
2 tablespoons cashew
  nuts, fried or roasted
  until golden brown
2 tablespoons mint
  leaves, chopped or
  whole

Serves 6
Preparation time: **45 mins**
Marinating time: **4 hours**
Cooking time: **25 mins**

1 To prepare the chicken, dry roast the fennel, white peppercorns, cumin and cardomom over low heat until aromatic, then grind to a powder. Put the chicken in a mixing bowl. Add the ground spice powder, ginger and garlic pastes, yoghurt and salt. Rub over the chicken and marinate in the refrigerator for 4 hours.

2 Heat ghee over medium flame and fry the cinnamon, cloves, cardamoms and bay leaves until aromatic. Add the green chillies and onion slices. Sauté until the onions soften and turn golden brown evenly, stirring continuously. Add tomatoes, turmeric, chilli powder, coriander powder and nutmeg powder. Sauté over low heat until oil separates and the tomato becomes soft and pulpy. Add the chicken and marinade. Stir to mix well and leave to cook for 3 to 5 minutes, until almost done.

3 To prepare the rice, heat the ghee over medium heat and fry the cinnamon, cardamoms, cloves, star anise and bay leaf until aromatic. Add rice and mix well until every grain is coated with ghee. Remove from heat.

4 Place cooked chicken into a rice cooker. Add rice and all remaining ingredients. When rice is ready, remove whole spices and fluff up rice. Garnish with fried cashew nuts, raisins and mint leaves.

Andhra Egg Biryani

2 tablespoons ghee
6 cardamoms
2 bay leaves
2 onions, sliced finely
4 cloves
2 ripe tomatoes, diced
6 eggs, hardboiled and
   shelled, four slits made
   on each without reach-
   ing the yolk
850 ml (3$^1/_3$ cups)
   water
500 g (2$^1/_4$ cups)
   Basmati rice or long
   grain rice, washed and
   drained

Spice paste
100 g (1 cup) grated
   coconut
2 medium onions, peeled
4 garlic cloves, peeled
3 cm (1 in) ginger,
   peeled
6 green chillies
100 g (2 cups) fresh
   coriander (cilantro)
   leaves, chopped,
   reserving 1 tablespoon
   for garnish
1 teaspoon garam masala
1 teaspoon chilli powder
125 ml ($^1/_2$ cup) yoghurt
2 teaspoons salt

1 Combine the spice paste ingredients in a blender and blend into a smooth paste.

2 In a deep pan, heat ghee over medium heat. Fry the cardamoms and bay leaves until aromatic. Add onions and fry for 2 to 3 minutes stirring continuously, until onions soften and turn evenly golden brown.

3 Add the diced tomatoes and blended spice paste to the pan and cook over low heat, until the oil separates and tomatoes are pulpy. Stir occasionally.

4 Add the eggs and fry until the eggs are coated with the mixture. Remove the eggs and set aside.

5 Add the water to the pan and bring to the boil. Add the drained rice and cook over low heat until all the water is absorbed and rice is tender. This takes about 20 to 25 minutes.

6 Cut the eggs into halves, place on top of the rice and garnish with reserved chopped coriander just before serving.

If you prefer a more spicy rice mixture, add one or two sliced green chillies when cooking the rice. Alternatively, you can serve the eggs separately from the rice.

Serves 6
Preparation time: 30 mins
Cooking time: 30 mins

Vegetable Biryani

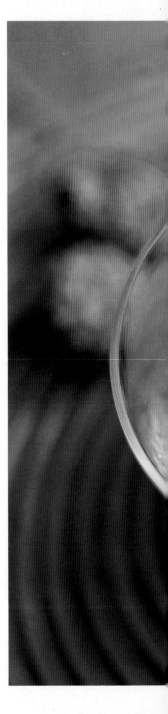

150 g (1 cup) mung lentils or red lentils
2 tablespoons ghee
5 cm (2 in) cinnamon stick, broken in half
6 cardamoms
6 cloves
3 bay leaves
2 medium onions, finely chopped
2 cm (1 in) ginger, finely minced
1 red chilli, thinly sliced
500 g ($2^1/_4$ cups) long grain rice, washed and drained
1 teaspoon curry powder
160 g (1 cup) green peas or diced mixed vegetables
1 litre (4 cups) water
$1^1/_2$ teaspoon salt

1 Dry roast mung lentils in a wok over medium heat for 3 to 5 minutes, or until aromatic and golden brown. Cool thoroughly. Wash well and drain, then set aside.

2 Heat ghee and fry cinnamon, cardamoms, cloves and bay leaves over medium heat until aromatic, 1 to 2 minutes.

3 Add onions, ginger and red chilli. Sauté until onions are light brown, 2 to 3 minutes.

4 Transfer to a rice cooker. Add the rest of the ingredients and mix well. Cook according to the manufacturer's instructions. When rice is cooked, fluff up rice with a wooden spoon. Serve with a salad or vegetable.

If a rice cooker is unavailable: Follow to Step 3. Bring water to a boil in a deep pot. Add in all the ingredients and mix well. Reduce heat to low, cover pot and gently simmer, stirring occasionally until rice is cooked and water, evaporated. This will take 20 to 25 minutes.

Serves 4
Preparation time: **20 mins**
Cooking time: **20 mins**

Lazeez Meat Biryani

Rice

1 litre (4 cups) lamb
  stock
2 tablespoons ghee
5 cm (2 in) cinnamon
  stick, broken in half
5 cardamoms
5 cloves
1 star anise
1 bay leaf
2 green chillies, slit
  lengthwise
500 g ($2^1/_4$ cups)
  basmati rice, washed
  and drained
125 ml ($^1/_2$ cup)
  yoghurt
2 tablespoons ginger
  paste
2 tablespoons garlic
  paste
$1^1/_4$ teaspoons salt
2 tablespoons chopped
  fresh coriander
  (cilantro) leaves
2 tablespoons chopped
  mint leaves

Lamb

3 tablespoons garlic paste
125 ml ($^1/_2$ cup) onion
  paste
3 tablespoons ginger paste
500 ml (2 cups) water
500 g (1 lb) boneless
  lamb, cubed
1 litre (4 cups) water
125 ml ($^1/_2$ cup) yoghurt
1 teaspoon salt
3 green chillies, slit
  lengthwise
1 teaspoon turmeric
  powder
1 tablespoon chilli powder
1 tablespoon coriander
  powder
1 teaspoon cumin powder
2 teaspoons garam masala
3 tomatoes, diced
2 cinnamon sticks
5 cardamoms
5 cloves
1 star anise
3 onions, diced
$1^1/_2$ teaspoons salt

Garnishes

3 tablespoons fried
  cashew nuts
3 tablespoons raisins
3 tablespoons finely
  chopped fresh
  coriander (cilantro)
  leaves (optional)
3 tablespoons finely
  chopped mint leaves
  (optional)
A generous pinch of
  saffron soaked in 250 ml
  (1 cup) hot milk mixed
  with 1 teaspoon *kewra*
  or rose essence

Serves 6
Preparation time: **45 mins**
Cooking time: **1 hour
  10 mins**

1 To prepare the rice, bring stock to the boil in a deep pan. Add remaining ingredients, stir to mix well, and cook, covered, over medium-low flame, stirring once or twice until the rice is cooked and the moisture evaporated, about 20 minutes.
2 To prepare the meat, put all the meat ingredients into a pot and boil over medium heat partially covered until the meat is tender and most of the liquid has evaporated, about 15 to 20 minutes. When meat is ready, remove the whole spices and set aside. Preheat oven to 160°C (325°F, gas mark 3).
3 To assemble the rice, fluff up the rice, place one-third of it on an oven-proof dish and arrange half of the cooked meat pieces on it. Sprinkle with half of cashew nuts, raisins, coriander and mint leaves. Top up with another third of the rice. Arrange the balance of the lamb pieces and sprinkle with the remaining half of the garnishes. Cover with the balance of rice. Drizzle saffron milk over the rice.
4 Cover the pot with aluminium foil, place in preheated oven for 1 hour. Serve hot.

Navarattan Pilau

2 tablespoons finely
  ground cashew nuts
3 tablespoons garlic paste
2 tablespoons ginger
  paste
1 1/2 tablespoons meat
  curry powder
3 tablespoons ghee
5 cm (2 in) cinnamon
  stick
5 cardamoms
5 cloves
2 bay leaves
2 large onions, finely
  sliced
300 g (1 1/2 cups)
  basmati rice, washed
  and drained
750 g (3 cups) mixed
  vegetables (cauliflower,
  French beans, carrots,
  peas, eggplant/
  aubergine)
2 tablespoons chopped
  mint leaves
2 tablespoons chopped
  fresh coriander
  (cilantro) leaves
2 green chillies, slit
  lengthwise
90 ml (1/3 cup) yoghurt
2 teaspoons salt
3 cups (750 ml) water
1 teaspoon yellow
  colouring

Garnishes
3 tablespoons cashew
  nuts, fried or roasted
  until golden brown
2 tablespoons raisins,
  fried in a little ghee
  until they puff up
30 g (3/4 cup) chopped
  fresh coriander
  (cilantro) leaves
30 g (3/4 cup) chopped
  mint leaves

Serves 5
Preparation time: 20 mins
Cooking time: 20 mins

1 Combine ground cashew nuts, garlic and ginger
pastes, and curry powder in a small bowl. Set aside.
2 Heat ghee. Fry cinnamon, cardamoms, cloves and bay
leaves over medium heat for about 1 minute, or until
aromatic. Add onion slices and fry for 2 to 3 minutes,
until onion softens and turns evenly golden brown,
stirring continuously. Add rice and stir to mix well.
Remove from heat.
3 Transfer to a rice cooker. Add the rest of the ingredients, including the reserved nut and paste mixture,
stir to mix well and turn on rice cooker.
4 When cooked, garnish with roasted cashew nuts,
fried raisins, chopped coriander and mint leaves.

Cauliflower Kofta Pilau

Cauliflower *Koftas*

500 g (1 lb) cauliflower
1 teaspoon salt
1 teaspoon garam masala
1 teaspoon turmeric
   powder
2 tablespoons finely
   chopped fresh coriander
   (cilantro) leaves
Oil for deep-frying

Spice Paste

3 tablespoons grated
   coconut
3 cm (1 in) ginger
5 cloves garlic
3 green chillies
2 red chillies
2 teaspoons coriander
   seeds
5 cardamoms
3 cloves
1 teaspoon black
   peppercorns
3 sprigs curry leaves
3 tablespoons fresh
   coriander (cilantro)
   leaves
125 ml ($^1/_2$ cup) yoghurt

Rice

3 tablespoons ghee
4 cloves garlic with skin,
   lightly crushed
3 medium onions, thinly
   sliced
500 g ($2^1/_4$ cups)
   Basmati rice, washed
   and drained
875 ml ($3^1/_2$ cups) water
2 teaspoons salt

1 To prepare the cauliflower *koftas*, cut the cauliflowers into big florets, then steam them for 3 to 4 minutes. When cool, mash with the rest of the *kofta* ingredients. Mix well and shape into small balls.

2 Heat oil and deep-fry the cauliflower balls until golden brown, then drain on absorbent paper.

3 Blend spice paste ingredients to a smooth paste.

4 Heat ghee over medium flame and fry the garlic and onion slices until soft and golden brown. Add the washed and drained rice and mix well.

5 Add the spice paste, water and salt. Cook over low heat until the rice is cooked and the moisture absorbed, about 20 minutes.

6 Add cauliflower *koftas* just before serving.

Serves 6
Preparation time: **40 mins**
Cooking time: **20 mins**

Tomato Chicken Pilau

1¹/₄ litres (5 cups) water
125 ml (¹/₂ cup) yoghurt
500 g (2¹/₄ cups) Basmati rice or long grain rice,
  washed and drained
1 kg (2 lb) chicken, cut into 10 pieces
3 medium onions, chopped into long slices
8 green chilies, slit lengthwise
5 medium tomatoes, sliced thinly
A pinch of saffron or 1 teaspoon turmeric powder
2 tablespoons ghee
2¹/₂ teaspoons salt
1 tablespoon curry powder
2 tablespoons finely chopped fresh coriander
  (cilantro) leaves
2 tablespoons finely chopped mint leaves
1 tablespoon finely chopped spring onion (scallion)
6 cloves
6 cardamoms
5 cm (2 in) cinnamon stick, broken in half
2 tablespoons coriander seeds, coarsely pounded
2 tablespoons garlic paste
2 tablespoons ginger paste

1 Bring water and yoghurt to the boil in a deep, heavy bottomed pan.
2 Add the rest of the ingredients, and stir to mix well. Cover and leave it to cook over medium heat until the chicken is cooked and the water evaporated, about 25 minutes.
3 Remove whole spices before serving.

Serves 6
Preparation time: **30 mins**
Cooking time: **25 mins**

Potato-stuffed Fried Flaky Bread
(Aloo Paratha)

Paratha

250 g (2 cups) plain
flour
50 ml ($^1/_5$ cup) milk
10 teaspoons yoghurt
60 ml ($^1/_4$ cup) water
1 tablespoon ghee or
butter
$^1/_2$ teaspoon salt

Stuffing

200 g (2 cups) potatoes,
boiled and mashed
2 green chillies, finely
chopped
3 tablespoons finely
chopped fresh coriander
(cilantro) leaves
1 medium onion, finely
chopped
1 teaspoon salt
$^1/_2$ teaspoon carom
seeds (*ajwain*)

1 Put all the ingredients for making the *paratha* into a mixing bowl and mix, then knead well until you form a pliable dough. Divide into 4 equal portions and shape into balls.

2 Mix all the stuffing ingredients thoroughly. Divide into 4 portions.

3 Flatten a piece of dough slightly. Put a portion of the filling on it and roll up to enclose the filling. Place this on a lightly floured surface and roll out into a thin circle, about 1 cm ($^1/_2$ in) thick.

4 Heat a lightly greased shallow frying pan. Place a stuffed *paratha* on it and cook for 5 minutes over medium heat on one side and then flip to cook the other side for 5 minutes.

To cook cauliflower paratha, simply substitute cauliflower for the potato, but squeeze out all the moisture before adding it to the other ingredients in step 2.

Serves 4
Preparation time: **30 mins**
Cooking time: **30 mins**

Shape dough into 4 balls.

Mix all stuffing ingredients thoroughly and divide into 4 portions.

Spicy Potato-stuffed Pancake (Masala Thosai)

1 cup (170 g) white gram
80 g (¹/₂ cup) short grain rice
360 g (2 cups) parboiled rice
500 ml (2 cups) water
³/₄ teaspoon salt

Stuffing
2 tablespoons oil or ghee
1 teaspoon white gram
1 dried chilli, cut into 2-cm (³/₄-in) pieces
¹/₂ teaspoon mustard seeds
¹/₂ teaspoon cumin seeds
2 large onions, diced
2 green chillies, sliced
2 cloves garlic, minced
2 cm (³/₄ in) ginger, minced
2 sprigs curry leaves
500 g (1 lb) potatoes, scrubbed and boiled until cooked, peeled and diced
1 teaspoon turmeric powder
1¹/₂ teaspoon salt

1 Wash the white gram, rice and parboiled rice and soak for 5 hours. Drain then combine with the 500 ml (2 cups) water and salt and blend until smooth.

2 Allow this batter to ferment overnight or for about 12 hours at room temperature (28°C). If the batter is fermented on a relatively warm day, you may have to reduce standing time.

3 Heat oil or ghee over medium flame and fry the white gram until golden brown. Add the dried chilli, mustard seeds and the cumin seeds and fry until aromatic.

4 Add in the onions, green chillies, garlic, ginger and curry leaves. Sauté until onions soften and brown evenly; stir continuously.

5 Add in the diced potatoes, turmeric powder and salt and mix well. Remove from heat.

6 When the batter has fermented. Heat and grease a flat pan over medium heat. Take a ladle full of batter and spread it thinly on the pan with the ladle. Cook for 2 minutes or until it becomes golden brown. Turn over and cook other side.

7 Place 2 tablespoons of the prepared potato on the thosai and fold first one side and then the other over it. Remove from the pan and serve immediately.

Makes 10 pieces
Soaking time: **5 hours**
Preparation time: **20 mins**
Fermentation time: **12 hours**
Cooking time: **20 mins**

Sauté the spices and onions, then add the potatoes and mix well.

Place 2 tablespoons filling onto the pancake, then fold to wrap.

Plain Pancake
(Atta Thosai)

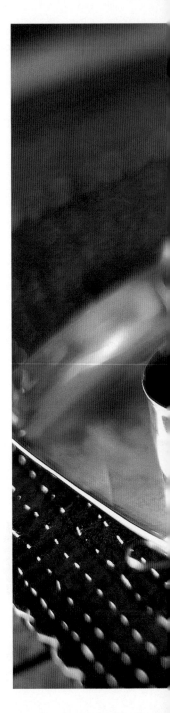

225 g (1¹/₄ cup) wheat flour (*atta*)
450 ml (1³/₄ cups) thick coconut milk (add 1 cup water
  if using canned or packet coconut)
¹/₂ teaspoon salt
1 egg
Ghee or butter for greasing

1 Put the flour, coconut milk, salt and egg into a
blender and blend until lump free.
2 Lightly grease a frying pan or hotplate with ghee or
butter. Heat frying pan or hot plate over medium
heat. When pan is hot, scoop up a ladleful of batter,
pour it on the hotplate. Quickly spread batter into a
thin pancake with the back of the ladle.
3 When light brown spots appear on the underside,
after about 1 to 2 minutes, flip to cook the other side.
4 Fold it into two and place on a serving plate. Serve
with date chutney or a chutney of your choice.

Serves 5
Preparation time: **20 mins**
Cooking time: **20 mins**

Onion Pancake
(Rangeela Uttappam)

240 g (2 cups) plain flour
120 g (1 cup) rice flour
50 g ($^1/_2$ cup) Bengal gram flour
2 teaspoons cumin seeds
500 ml (2 cups) tomato juice
90 g (1 cup) coarsely grated carrot
2 medium onions, sliced thinly
2 green chillies, sliced
2 tablespoons finely chopped fresh coriander
  (cilantro) leaves
2 teaspoons salt
500 ml (2 cups) water
Oil for shallow-frying

1 Mix all ingredients well to make a thick batter.
2 Heat a flat non-stick pan and grease it lightly with oil.
3 Take a big ladle full of batter and spread it evenly on the pan in a circular movement. The pancake should be about 10 cm (4 in) wide and $^1/_2$ cm ($^1/_4$ in) thick.
4 Fry pancake over medium heat for 2 to 4 minutes on each side, or until crisp and golden brown.

Makes 12 pieces
Preparation time: **15 mins**
Cooking time: **40 mins**

Garlic Naan

2 large eggs
250 ml (1 cup) milk
1 tablespoon caster sugar
125 ml ($^1/_2$ cup) oil
1 teaspoon salt
1 teaspoon instant yeast
500 g (4 cups) plain flour sifted with $^1/_2$ teaspoon
  baking powder
Water
1 teaspoon ghee or butter to brush on *naan*
6 cloves garlic, minced
2 tablespoons chopped fresh coriander
  (cilantro) leaves

1 Mix together eggs, milk, sugar, oil, and salt, and beat
until the sugar dissolves. Add the mixture and instant
yeast to the sifted flour and knead the dough, occasionally
adding some water until dough is soft and fluffy.
2 Cover dough with a damp cloth and set aside for
15 minutes before kneading it again. Cover and leave
it again, this time for about 2 hours. After 2 hours,
divide the dough into five portions.
3 Preheat oven to 230°C (445°F, gas mark 8).
4 On a lightly floured surface, flatten the dough by
pressing it out by hand until the dough is about 1 cm
($^1/_2$ in) thin.
5 Brush with butter or ghee and sprinkle with garlic
and chopped coriander.
6 Place onto a lightly greased baking tray and bake in
the oven for 3 to 5 minutes on each side, or until fluffy
and light brown.

Makes 5 pieces
Preparation time: **3 hours**
Cooking time: **15 mins**

Kashmiri Naan

360 g (3 cups) self-raising flour
1 teaspoon salt
1/2 teaspoon baking soda
1 tablespoon oil
2 tablespoons butter
6 tablespoons plain natural yoghurt
1/2 teaspoon instant yeast
3–4 tablespoons warm milk for kneading
100 g (2/3 cup) mixed dried fruits, chopped (raisins, dates, cherries)

Makes 8 pieces
Preparation time: **2 hours**
Fermentation time: **6 hours**
Cooking time: **25 mins**

1 Sieve together the self-raising flour, salt and baking soda into a large bowl. Add oil, butter, yoghurt and instant yeast, and rub in with your fingers.

2 When the dough resembles course breadcrumbs, add milk, a little at a time, until a soft pliable dough is formed. Cover and set aside for 5 to 6 hours to ferment at room temperature (28°C). If the dough is fermented on a relatively warm day, you may have to reduce standing time.

3 After 5 to 6 hours, knead dough lightly, adding a little warm milk if necessary, and divide into 8 portions.

4 On a lightly floured surface, roll out a piece of dough into a $1/2$-cm ($1/4$-in) thick piece. Sprinkle with some chopped fruits and roll lightly so that the fruits are embedded. Then, using a rolling pin, lightly roll it to flatten it a little.

5 Heat a hot plate, or heavy-based pan, until very hot. Lightly grease the hot plate or pan. Drizzle a little water on the top of the *naan* with your hands.

6 Invert the *naan* and place it to the hot plate or pan. Cook over high heat on both sides until brown specks appear.

This recipe is a variation of traditional Kashmiri Naan recipes, in which the fruits were sandwiched between two pieces of dough.

Ceylonese Roti with Spicy Onion Chutney

Ceylonese Roti

120 g (3 cups) plain flour
$1/2$ teaspoon baking
  powder
1 teaspoon salt
100 g (1 cup) grated
  coconut
150 ml ($2/3$ cup) water
Oil or ghee for shallow-
  frying

Makes 8 pieces
Preparation time: 40 mins
Cooking time: 30 mins

Spicy Onion Chutney

4 large onions (400 g)
2 medium tomatoes
15 dried chillies (12 g)
2 tablespoons oil
1 teaspoon mustard seeds
1 sprig curry leaves
50 g ($1 2/3$ oz) tamarind
  mixed with 100ml
  (scant $1/2$ cup) water
  and strained
$1/2$ cup (125 ml) water
$1 1/2$ teaspoons salt

Serves 4
Preparation time: 15 mins
Cooking time: 5 mins

1 To make the roti, put flour, baking powder, salt, and coconut into a bowl. Mix well.

2 Slowly add in the water and knead to form a soft dough. Set aside covered for 30 minutes, then divide dough into 8 portions.

3 Roll out each portion of dough into a circle of 12 cm (5 in) diameter and $1/2$ cm ($1/4$ in) thickness. Sprinkle with more flour if the dough is sticky.

4 Heat a frying pan and grease it lightly. Cook the roti over low heat until brown specks appear, about 2 to 3 minutes on each side.

5 To make the chutney, peel and cube onions and slice the tomatoes.

6 Soak the dried chillies in water for 15 minutes and drain.

7 Heat oil and fry the mustard seeds and curry leaves until aromatic. Add in the cubed onions, tomatoes and the soaked dried chillies. Saute for 2 minutes until tomatoes become pulpy.

8 Remove from heat and set aside.

9 Mix tamarind in the water and strain. Put sautéed ingredients, tamarind water and salt into a food processor and blend till smooth.

Sheermal

2 cups (240 g) plain
  flour, sifted with
  1 teaspoon salt
2 teaspoons instant yeast
1 tablespoon caster sugar
3 tablespoons butter
2 tablespoons yoghurt
125 ml ($^1/_2$ cup) warm
  milk
2 tablespoons raisins
$^1/_4$ teaspoon saffron
  strands soaked in
  2 tablespoons hot milk

Makes 5 pieces
Preparation time: **30 mins**
Fermentation time:
  12 hours
Cooking time: **10 mins**

1 Combine the flour, yeast, sugar, butter, yoghurt and milk in a mixing bowl and and knead to form a soft pliable dough. The dough should be fairly sticky.
2 Keep the dough in a deep bowl covered with a plate. Set the dough aside for 12 hours to ferment at room temperature (28°C). If the dough is fermented on a relatively warm day, you may have to reduce standing time.
3 After 12 hours, divide into 5 portions. Roll them out on a floured surface into $1^1/_2$-cm ($^3/_4$-in) thick round breads with the centre thinner than the edges and place on a greased baking tray.
4 Preheat oven to 250°C (480°F, gas mark 9).
5 Sprinkle some raisins and saffron milk over the sheermal and bake for 10 minutes or until golden brown.

Roll out each portion of dough into $1^1/_2$-cm ($^3/_4$-in) thick circles.

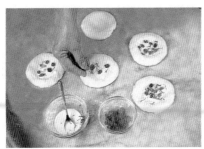

Sprinkle raisins and saffron milk over the sheermal before baking.

Deep-fried Spiced Bread (Methi Puri)

2 tablespoons ghee or oil

210 g (2 cups) wheat flour (*atta*)

2 tablespoons dried fenugreek leaves

3 tablespoons finely chopped fresh coriander (cilantro) leaves

1 1/2 teaspoons chilli powder

1 teaspoon cumin seeds

1/2 teaspoon asafoetida powder

1/2 teaspoon turmeric powder

1 teaspoon salt

180 ml (3/4 cup) water

Oil for deep-frying

1 Rub the ghee into the flour until the mixture resembles fine breadcrumbs.

2 Add the rest of the ingredients, except for the oil, and mix and knead to form a soft pliable dough. Keep the dough covered for 15 minutes

3 Divide dough into 6 portions and roll out each portion into a thin circle.

4 Heat oil for deep-frying and fry in very hot oil for 1 to 2 minutes on each side, or until light brown

Makes 6 pieces
Preparation time: **25 mins**
Cooking time: **20 mins**

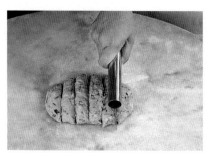

Divide dough into six portions.

Roll each portion into a thin circle.

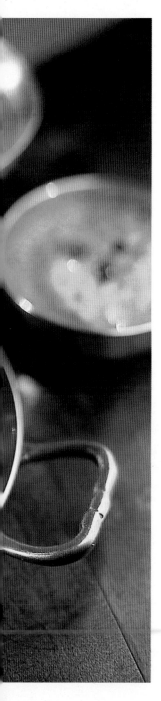

Deep-fried Puffed Bread
(Batura)

240 g (2 cups) plain flour
$1/2$ teaspoon bicarbonate of soda
$1/2$ teaspoon salt
2 tablespoons yoghurt
2 tablespoons ghee
125 ml ($1/2$ cup) milk
Oil for deep-frying

1 Sieve together flour, bicarbonate of soda and salt into a mixing bowl.
2 Add the rest of the ingredients and knead to form a soft, pliable dough. Cover the bowl with a damp cloth and set aside for 6 hours to ferment at room temperature (28°C). If the dough is fermented on a relatively warm day, you may have to reduce standing time.
3 Knead the dough again. Divide dough into five portions. Roll into circles about $1/2$ cm ($1/4$ in) thick and 13 cm (5 in) in diameter.
4 Heat oil for deep-frying and fry the *batura*, one at a time, in very hot oil. When one side of the *batura* turns light golden in colour, carefully turn it over and fry the other side until it turns light golden in colour as well.

Makes 5 pieces
Preparation time: **10 minutes**
Fermentation time: **6 hours**
Cooking time: **2–3 mins per batura**

Index